Instant Pot Cookbook

Simple Pressure Cooker Recipes for Busy People*

*including breakfast and dessert recipes

by Katy Adams

Table of Contents

INTRODUCTION 4

BREAKFAST RECIPES 7

    QUICK & EASY RICE PUDDING WITH CINNAMON AND RAISIN 7

    SIMPLE HARD BOILED BREAKFAST EGGS 9

    CUBAN EGG POTATO FRITTATA 11

    BANANA & CREAM ROLLED OATS 13

SIDE DISHES 15

    RED POTATOES WITH PARMESAN 15

    CHEESY MASHED POTATOES 17

    JUICY VEGGIES WITH HAM 19

    PRESSURE COOKER BROWN RICE 21

    MEXICAN STYLE STUFFED PEPPERS 23

MAIN DISHES 25

    ITALIAN SHREDDED BEEF 25

    SWEET AND JUICY RUSSIAN CHICKEN 27

    BEEF RISOTTO BOLOGNESE 29

    CORNED BEEF WITH CABBAGE 31

    CURRY BEEF STEW 33

    PRESSURE COOKER CHILI MEAT BEANS 35

    MELT-IN-MOUTH PRESSURE COOKER RIBS 37

SOUPS 39

    CREAMY LEEK SOUP 39

    PRESSURE COOKER PEA SOUP 41

    PRESSURE COOKER BBS (BEEF BARLEY SOUP) 43

    CLASSIC LENTIL SOUP 45

    HOMEMADE CHICKEN SOUP 47

DESSERT RECIPES 49

    DELICIOUS EGG CUSTARD 49

    MOUTH-WATERING CINNAMON APPLE PULL APART BREAD 51

    5-MINUTE DELICIOUS APPLESAUCE 53

    Simple Caramel Flan 55
COOKING MEASUREMENT CONVERSIONS **57**
CONCLUSION..**60**

Introduction

I want to start by thanking you for downloading my book "***Instant Pot Cookbook: Simple Pressure Cooker Recipes for Busy People***". I am very pleased that thanks to my book, you will plunge into the world of quick, simple & delicious Pressure Cooker Recipes!

Electric Pressure Cooker is a special kitchen appliance for cooking food with the help of water or other cooking liquids. The pressure inside the pot is created by boiling water, broth or other liquid. The steam inside the cooker increases the internal pressure and raise the temperature. This helps food to cook quicker than in usual pot or slow cooker. By the way, this way of cooking has one great benefit: pressure cooker food cooks faster than other cooking methods, so it can save energy and your money!

After preparation, you may use quick or slow pressure release method to reduce pressure and open the lid safety.

A pressure cooker can be easily used for a quick stewing and almost any food can be prepared in this amazing kitchen appliance.

Modern pressure cookers have portable design and consist of basic components: the pan itself, with two pan handles on opposite ends, the lid which usually includes:

- Lid handle with locking device

- Sealing ring
- Steam vent with pressure regulator
- Pressure indicator pin
- Over-temperature pressure release valves
- Pressure gauge (usually absent but included on some costlier models)

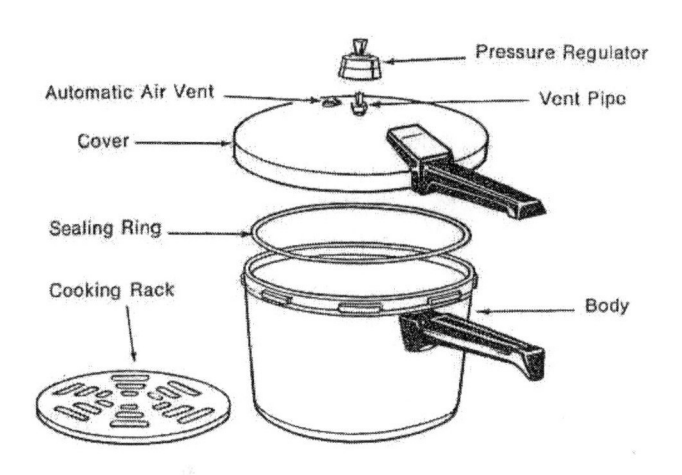

Also, pressure cooker devices provides with different accessories, which can make food cooking more convenient:

- Steamer basket
- Trivet for keeping the steamer basket above liquid
- Metal divider, for separating vegetables or other foods in the steamer basket.

The list of parts and accessories may differ slightly depending on the manufacturer and model of a pressure cooker.

This cookbook contains most popular Electric pressure cooker recipes to make you life tastier and healthier. Dip into the delicious and mouth-watering meals and improve your cooking skills with pleasure! **Clean the dust from your Pressure Cooker and let's begin!**

Breakfast recipes

Quick & Easy Rice Pudding with Cinnamon and Raisin

Preparation time: 4 minutes, cooking time: 5-7 minutes, servings: 5-6

Ingredients

- 1 cup Arborio Rice
- 1½ cups water
- 2½ cups skimmed milk
- 3 tablespoon sugar
- 1 cinnamon stick
- 2 large eggs, beaten
- ½ teaspoon vanilla extract, optional
- ½ cup raisins
- A pinch of salt
- Cinnamon for garnish

Directions

1. In your Pressure Cooker cooking pot, pour in water and add rice, cinnamon stick and salt.
2. Lock the lid and close Pressure Valve. Cook on High Pressure for 4 minutes.
3. When ready, apply a 10 minute natural pressure release and then do a quick release to remove the remaining pressure.
4. Open lid and add 2 cups of the skimmed milk and sugar to the pressure cooking pot and combine evenly.
5. Then in the large mixing bowl beat the eggs and vanilla, add the remaining milk and whisk well to combine.
6. Slowly pour the mixture into the pressure cooker.
7. Select the Sauté function and bring pudding to come to a slow boil, stirring constantly. Continue to whisk for one minute only.
8. Remove cooking pot from Pressure Cooker, add raisins and mix together.
9. Serve with additional raisins and nuts if desired, sprinkled with cinnamon and nutmeg.

Simple Hard Boiled Breakfast Eggs

Preparation time: 1 minute, cooking time: 2-3 minutes, *(handwritten: 6-7 minutes)*
servings: 5

Ingredients

- 10 large eggs
- 1 cup water
- A pinch of salt
- Steamer basket

(handwritten: 4-5 min. natural release)

Directions

1. Pour one cup of water into the Pressure Cooker cooking pot.
2. Place basket of eggs into Pressure Cooker cooking pot.
3. Lock on lid and cook at high pressure for 2 minutes.
4. When timer beeps, use a natural pressure release method.
5. Peel eggs, season with salt slightly and enjoy light and healthy breakfast.

Cuban Egg Potato Frittata

Preparation time: 10 minutes, cooking time: 10-12 minutes, servings: 3-4

Ingredients

- 2-3 medium-sized potatoes, peeled and sliced
- 6 large eggs
- 1 tablespoon butter, melted
- 1 medium-sized onion, diced
- 4 oz cheese, grated plus 1 oz grated cheese for topping
- 1 teaspoon Italian seasoning
- 1 clove garlic, minced
- 2 tablespoons baking mix
- ¼ cup skimmed milk
- 1 teaspoon tomato paste
- 1 - 1/2 cups water
- ½ teaspoon salt
- ¼ teaspoon black pepper, freshly ground

Directions

1. Peel and slice potatoes into thin strips and soak in water for 20 minutes.
2. Meanwhile, in a medium bowl, whisk together eggs and seasonings until very frothy.
3. In another mixing bowl, combine together baking mix, tomato paste and milk. Then add to egg mixture. Stir to combine. Add onions and garlic to egg mixture.
4. Thoroughly grease casserole dish.
5. Remove potatoes from water and dry with a kitchen towel. Add potatoes and pour in melted butter. Pour in egg mixture and top with grated cheese.
6. Add water to Pressure Cooker cooking pot and place a Trivet. Place casserole on Trivet.
7. Lock on lid and close Pressure Valve.
8. Cook on High Pressure for 10-12 minutes.
9. When ready, use a 5 minute natural pressure release and then release the rest of the pressure.
10. Top additionally with grated cheese and place lid on top of pressure cooker to get the cheese melted.

Banana & Cream Rolled Oats

Preparation time: 3 minutes, cooking time: 12-15 minutes, servings: 2

Ingredients

- 1 cup rolled oats
- 1 - ½ cup whole milk
- 1 large banana
- 1 pinch salt
- 1 teaspoon sugar

Directions

1. Pour 2 cups of water into the pressure cooker and set the steamer basket.
2. In a small heat-proof bowl or mug, add the oats, milk, and salt. Close and lock the lid of the pressure cooker and cook for 10 minutes at high pressure.
3. When time is up, open the pressure cooker using the natural release method
4. Cut the banana and add to the bowl.

5. Vigorously mix the contents of the bowl, sprinkle with sugar and serve.

Side Dishes

Red Potatoes with Parmesan

Preparation time: 5 minutes, cooking time: 10 minutes, servings: 4

Ingredients

- 4 medium-sized red potatoes, unpeeled and quartered
- 3 teaspoons garlic powder
- 1 can (14-1/2 ounces) chicken broth
- 2 tablespoons minced fresh parsley
- 1/3 cup grated Parmesan cheese

Directions

1. Cut potatoes into quarters and place in a pressure cooker. Sprinkle with cheese and garlic powder, pour in chicken broth.

2. Close cover securely and place pressure regulator on vent pipe. Bring cooker to full pressure over high heat and cook for 6 minutes.
3. When ready, use a natural pressure release for about 10 minutes or until it completely reduced.
4. Sprinkle with parsley and additional parmesan cheese.

Cheesy Mashed Potatoes

Preparation time: 12 minutes, cooking time: 15 minutes, servings: 3-4

Ingredients

- 4-6 large russet potatoes, peeled and quartered
- 1 cup water
- 4 oz milk
- 2 tablespoon unsalted butter
- 2 cloves garlic, crushed
- 2 tablespoon Parmesan cheese, grated
- A pinch of salt
- Ground black pepper to taste
- Chopped dill or parsley for garnish (optional)

Directions

1. Pour in 1 cup of water in the pressure cooker.
2. Put the steamer trivet in the pot, place quartered potatoes in the steamer trivet. Close the lid and cook in high pressure for 8 minutes.

3. Meanwhile, the potatoes are preparing, melt the butter in a small sauce pan over medium heat. Add crushed garlic, season with salt and black pepper and sauté for 1 - 2 minutes until fragrant and golden in color. Add the milk and deglaze the pan. Remove the mixture from heat when it becomes hot.
4. When the timer beeps, use a natural release to drop the pressure. Uncover the pressure cooker. In the large mixing bowl mash potatoes with the help of potato masher. Pour in half of the garlic butter mixture and continue to mash. Stir to combine, and add the mixture until desired consistency.
5. Add grated Parmesan cheese. Add salt and pepper to taste and serve warm. Garnish mashed potatoes with finely chopped fresh parsley or dill if desired.

Juicy Veggies with Ham

Preparation time: 5 minutes, cooking time: 5-7 minutes, servings: 4-5

Ingredients

- 1 pound cooked ham steak
- 4 medium-sized potatoes, cut into 1-inch cubes
- 4 cups fresh green beans, cut
- 3 medium-sized carrots, halved widthwise
- 1 cup chicken broth
- 1 teaspoon onion powder
- ½ teaspoon salt
- Ground black pepper to taste

Directions

1. Place cooking rack in your pressure cooker. Add the potatoes, beans, carrots, broth, onion and salt. Place ham over vegetables. Close cover securely and bring the cooker to a full pressure. Cook for 5 minutes.
2. When timer beeps, use a nature pressure release.

3. Serve hot and enjoy!

Pressure Cooker Brown Rice

Preparation time: 5 minutes, cooking time: 15 minutes, servings: 4-6

Ingredients

- 2 cups long brown rice
- 4 cups water
- 4 chicken bouillon cubes
- 3 dashes Mrs. Dash seasoning mix, original
- 3 tablespoons butter
- 1 tablespoon olive oil
- Salt and black pepper to taste

Directions

1. Sprinkle the pressure cooker with olive oil. Load all ingredients to pressure cooker and lock the lid. Set the cooker to a high pressure and cook for 15 minutes.
2. When finished, use a natural pressure release to drop it down.

3. Serve brown rice as a side dish for any meat you prefer.

Mexican Style Stuffed Peppers

Preparation time: 10 minutes, cooking time: 15 minutes, servings: 4-5

Ingredients

- 4-5 large green, red or orange bell peppers
- 1 pound lean beef, ground
- 1 egg, beaten
- 1 cup salsa
- 1-1/2 cups crushed tortilla chips
- 1 medium-sized onion, chopped
- 2 tablespoon fresh cilantro, minced
- 1 red chili pepper, cored and finely chopped
- 3 garlic cloves, minced
- 2 teaspoon ground cumin
- 1/2 cup shredded Mexican cheese blend
- Sour cream for topping (optional)

Directions

1. Trim tops off of peppers and remove seeds.

2. In a large mixing bowl, combine the egg, salsa, crushed chips, onion, cilantro, chili pepper, garlic and cumin. Crumble beef over mixture and mix well. Then spoon into peppers.
3. Pour 1 - ½ cups water into your pressure cooker. Place peppers on steamer tray in pressure cooker; top with a piece of foil. Close cover securely according to manufacturer's directions and bring cooker to full pressure. Cook for 10 minutes.
4. When timer beeps, allow the pressure drop naturally
5. Remove peppers from the pressure cooker and sprinkle with cheese mixture.
6. Serve with sour cream and additional salsa if desired.

Main Dishes

Italian Shredded Beef
Preparation time: 5 minutes, cooking time: 50-60 minutes, servings: 6-8

Ingredients

- 3-4 pound beef chuck roast
- 10-15 oz beef stock
- 2 tablespoon Italian seasoning
- 2 garlic cloves, minced
- ¼ cup Water
- 16 pepperoncini peppers with juices
- 1 teaspoon salt
- ½ teaspoon black pepper, ground

Directions

1. Place beef chuck roast to the pressure cooker and season with Italian seasoning, salt and black

pepper. Pour in beef stock, water and add garlic and pepperoncini peppers with juices.
2. Lock on lid and close Pressure Valve. Cook at High Pressure for 55 minutes.
3. When becomes ready use a full natural pressure release.
4. Remove meat from pot and shred well using forks.
5. Return the meat to the pot to mix in with the juice.
6. Serve with cooker rice or mashed potatoes.

Sweet and Juicy Russian Chicken

Preparation time: 10 minutes, cooking time: 7 minutes, servings: 4-6

Ingredients

- 4-6 chicken breasts, boneless and skinless
- 1 bottle (16 oz) Russian dressing
- 1 jar (16 oz) Apricot Preserves
- 1 packet Lipton Onion Soup Mix
- ¼ cup water

Directions

1. In the large mixing bowl combine Russian dressing, apricot preserves and Lipton Onion Soup Mix.
2. Add water to your Pressure Cooker and place chicken breasts in it. Pour the mixture over the chicken.
3. Lock on Lid and cook at high pressure for 6 minutes.
4. When finish use a natural pressure release for 10-12 minutes.
5. Remove chicken to a plate.

6. Select Sauté or Browning and simmer until the sauce has thickened. Plate chicken and pour sauce on top.
7. You may also sprinkle the chicken with freshly chopped herbs like dill or parsley.

Beef Risotto Bolognese

Preparation time: 10 minutes, cooking time: 30 minutes, yields: 6-8

Ingredients

- 1 pound ground beef
- 6 slices of bacon, diced
- 1 medium-sized onion, diced
- 1 large carrot, diced
- 2 garlic cloves, minced
- 2 cups risotto rice (I prefer Arborio)
- ½ cup marsala
- 5 cups beef broth, divided
- 1 can (14.5 oz) diced tomatoes
- 1 tablespoon tomato paste
- 1 tablespoon olive oil
- 2 tablespoon milk
- 2 bay leaves
- 1/3 cup Parmesan, freshly grated + extra to serve
- Handful of fresh parsley, chopped
- A pinch of salt and pepper to taste

Directions

1. Heat the olive oil in your pressure cooker and brown the ground beef for about 4-6 minutes, stirring occasionally. Remove to a plate.
2. Add bacon to the pressure cooking pot and cook until crisp. Then add onions, carrots, and garlic, sauté until tender, about 3-4 minutes.
3. Add rice and cook, stirring frequently, until rice becomes opaque, about 3-4 minutes.
4. Add the marsala and cook 2 minutes. Pour in 4 cups beef broth, tomatoes, tomato paste, milk, bay leaves, and cooked ground beef. Cover and lock lid in place. Select High Pressure and set 6 minutes timer. After 6 minutes, turn off the pressure cooker and use a quick pressure release.
5. Select Simmer and stir in remaining 1 cup of beef broth. Cook uncovered, stirring occasionally for 2-3 minutes until most of the broth is absorbed and the rice is creamy.
6. Stir in grated Parmesan and chopped parsley. Season with salt and pepper to taste.
7. Serve hot with extra Parmesan on top.

Corned Beef with Cabbage
Preparation time: 10 minutes, cooking time: 45 minutes, servings: 5-6

Ingredients

- 2 pound corned beef brisket
- Corned beef spice packet
- 1 medium head cabbage, cut into 8 wedges
- 2 large red potatoes, cut into 2-inch cubes
- 5 medium-sized carrots, cut into 2-inch chunks
- 1 medium onion, roughly diced
- 1 can (14 oz) chicken broth
- 4 cups water

Directions

1. In pressure cooker pot, combine water and contents of corned beef seasoning packet. Add beef. Close cover securely and bring cooker to a high pressure. Cook for 45 minutes.
2. Meanwhile, in a large saucepan, combine the cabbage, potatoes and broth. Bring to a boil over

the high heat. Reduce heat, cover and simmer for 10 minutes. Add carrots and diced onion. Cover with a lid and simmer additionally 20-25 minutes or until vegetables are tender. When ready, drain well.
3. When the meat ready, use a natural pressure release to drop the pressure. Remove beef to a serving platter. Discard cooking liquid. Serve beef with cabbage and other veggies. You may also top the meat with freshly chopped parsley.

Curry Beef Stew

Preparation time: 10 minutes, cooking time: 35-40 minutes, servings: 4-5

Ingredients

- 2 pounds lean beef, cut into 2-inch pieces
- 2 medium-sized onions, roughly chopped
- 1 cup assorted Mushrooms
- 3 medium-sized potatoes, quartered
- 5 carrots, cut into 2-inch pieces
- 2 tablespoon extra virgin olive oil
- 4 garlic cloves, minced
- 3 cups water
- 1 tablespoon Worcestershire sauce
- ½ medium-sized apple, grated
- 2 teaspoons salt
- Ground black pepper to taste
- ½ box of Curry Mix

Directions

1. Select Sauté settings on your Pressure Cooker and heat well. Sprinkle with the olive oil and lightly sauté the meat and onions.
2. Turn off Pressure Cooker and add in water, Worcestershire Sauce, garlic, salt, and apple
3. Lock lid and cook at high pressure for 35 minutes.
4. When ready, turn off the Pressure Cooker and use natural pressure release.
5. Remove the lid and drop in the curry blocks. Mix until melted. Add potatoes, carrots, mushrooms and stir to combine.
6. Lock lid and cook at high for 4 minutes.
7. When finish, release the pressure naturally for about 10 minutes.
8. Serve with cooker rice.

Pressure Cooker Chili Meat Beans

Preparation time: 10 minutes, cooking time: 15-20 minutes, servings: 4

Ingredients

- 1 pound ground beef or your may also use ground turkey
- 1 can (14.5 oz) tomato sauce
- 1 can (14.5 oz) Kidney beans, with juices
- 1 can (14.5 oz) Pinto beans, with juices
- 1 medium-sized onion, diced
- 1 can (4 oz) green chilies, diced
- 2 stalk celery, diced
- 2 medium-sized tomatoes, diced
- 1 teaspoon ground cumin
- 2 tablespoon chili powder
- 1 teaspoon ground black pepper
- 2 teaspoon salt
- 1 tablespoon olive oil
- 1 - ½ cup water

Directions

1. First of all, prepare everything for further cooking: chop vegetables, combine spices and open all cans.
2. Select Sauté on your Pressure Cooker and heat well. Sprinkle the pressure cooker with olive oil and add ground meat. Break up the meat until it is totally crumbled.
3. Add the celery and onions and sauté for about two minutes. Then, add the rest of the ingredients.
4. Lock on Lid and cook on High for 20 minutes.
5. When ready, use a full natural pressure release.
6. You may simmer for two minutes to reduce come of the liquid, if desired.

Melt-in-Mouth Pressure Cooker Ribs
Preparation time: 5 minutes, cooking time: 20 minutes, servings: 4-6

Ingredients

- 2 pounds country-style pork ribs, boneless and cut into 2-inch chunks
- 1 medium-sized onion, diced
- 3 tablespoons ketchup
- 4-1/2 teaspoons white vinegar
- 1 teaspoon Worcestershire sauce
- 1 teaspoon prepared mustard
- 1 teaspoon ground black pepper
- 1 teaspoon paprika
- 1 tablespoon canola oil
- 1 cup water
- 1/8 teaspoon celery seed

Directions

1. First of all you need to prepare the meat. Sprinkle the ribs with the salt, pepper and paprika.

2. Using the Sauté mode in your pressure cooker, brown ribs in oil on all sides. Remove from the pressure cooker and drain fat. Return meat to the pressure cooker. Combine the remaining ingredients; pour over meat.
3. Close the lid securely and bring the cooker to full pressure over high heat. Reduce heat to medium-high and cook for 15 minutes.
4. Remove from the heat, use a nature pressure release.
5. Serve ribs with juices if desired.

Soups

Creamy Leek Soup

Preparation time: 25 minutes, cooking time: 10 minutes, servings: 6-8

Ingredients

- 4 bacon strips, diced
- 3 medium leeks (green ends trimmed), sliced
- 1 medium-sized onion, chopped
- 4 large potatoes, peeled and sliced
- 4 cups chicken broth
- 2 cups half-and-half cream
- 2 tablespoon fresh parsley, minced
- ½ tablespoon salt
- ½ teaspoon black pepper, freshly ground

Directions

1. Preheat your pressure cooker and cook bacon over medium heat until crisp. Remove with a slotted spoon to paper towels.
2. In the remaining bacon fat sauté leeks and onion until tender. Add potatoes and broth. Close cover securely and cook for 5 minutes.
3. When ready, use the natural pressure release for about 10 minutes. Uncover and cool soup slightly.
4. In a blender, process soup until smooth and return all to the pan. Add cream and parsley and heat over medium-low heat (do not bring to a boil).
5. Season with salt and pepper and garnish with bacon.

Pressure Cooker Pea Soup

Preparation time: 10 minutes, cooking time: 30 minutes, servings: 6-8

Ingredients

- 1 pound dried split peas
- 1 ham hock
- 1 medium-sized onion, diced
- 2 stalks celery, diced
- 8 cups water
- 1 teaspoon dried thyme
- 3 garlic cloves, minced
- 1 pinch ground black pepper
- 1 teaspoon salt
- 1 teaspoon hot pepper sauce (I prefer Tabasco)

Directions

1. Pour water into your pressure cooker. Add split peas, ham hock, diced onion, celery, thyme, minced garlic, and black pepper.

2. Close the pressure cooker lid securely and place pressure regulator over vent according to manufacturer's instructions. Bring to a high pressure and cook about 30 minutes.
3. When timer beeps, reduce the pressure using a natural pressure release.
4. Remove ham hock and strip off meat. Return meat to soup. Stir well to distribute flavors.
5. Season with salt and hot pepper sauce and serve hot. You may also top the soup with chopped parsley or cilantro.

Pressure Cooker BBS (Beef Barley Soup)
Preparation time: 10 minutes, cooking time: 35-40 minutes, servings: 6-8

Ingredients

- ¾ pound stew beef, cut into ½ - inch pieces
- 1 cup pearl barley, rinsed and drained
- 1 medium onion, diced
- ¼ cup celery, chopped
- 2 carrots, trimmed and diced
- 8 oz mushrooms, sliced
- 4 cups chicken broth
- 2 cups water
- 2 tablespoon vegetable oil
- 1 tablespoon dried thyme leaf
- 1 tablespoon tomato paste
- 1 tablespoon Worcestershire sauce
- ½ teaspoon fresh black pepper
- A pinch of salt to taste

Directions

1. Set the pressure cooker to Browning mode. Heat the vegetable oil in the cooker, and add the beef. Cook, stirring occasionally, until the meat is no longer pink, for about 3-4 minutes. Turn off the cooker, and remove the beef, leaving any excess oil in the pot.
2. Turn the cooker to Sauté mode. To the residual oil in the pot, add the onion, celery, carrots and mushrooms. Sauté, stirring frequently, until the onions are translucent and the mushrooms have given off some of their liquid, 3-4 minutes.
3. Add the thyme, tomato paste, Worcestershire sauce and black pepper. Stir until the mixture is fragrant (1-2 minutes). Add the barley and liquid, and the beef. Turn off the cooker.
4. Lock the lid of the pressure cooker. Set the timer for High Pressure for 10 minutes. When cooked, use the natural pressure release method, which will release the pressure in approximately 20 minutes.
5. When the pressure is released, ladle soup into individual serving bowls, and serve hot. Top with chopped parsley, dill or cilantro.

Classic Lentil Soup

Preparation time: 10 minutes, cooking time: 25 minutes, servings: 4-5

Ingredients

- 1 cup dry lentils, rinsed
- 1 small onion, finely chopped
- 4 garlic cloves, minced
- 2 small carrots, chopped
- 2 celery ribs, chopped
- 4 cups vegetable broth
- 2 bay leaves
- 2 tablespoons olive oil
- 1 teaspoon ground cumin
- A pinch of salt and pepper to taste

Directions

1. Preheat your pressure cooker, sprinkle with olive oil and sauté the onions and garlic until the onions are translucent. Add the carrots and celery and sauté for a minute or two.

2. Add the ground cumin and stir well. Add the vegetable broth, lentils, and bay leaves, close the pressure cooker lid, and bring up to a high pressure.
3. Cook for 20 minutes.
4. When ready, open the pressure cooker using the quick release method or let the pressure come down naturally.
5. Remove the bay leaves.
6. Season with salt and fresh ground pepper to taste and serve.

Homemade Chicken Soup

Preparation time: 10 minutes, cooking time: 8-10 minutes, servings: 6-8

Ingredients

- 1 pound breasts or chicken thighs, boneless
- 2 medium-sized carrots, chopped
- 1 medium-sized onion, chopped
- 1 cup frozen peas
- 1 cup frozen corn
- 2 celery stalks with leaves
- 6 cups chicken broth
- 2 tablespoon extra virgin olive oil
- ¼ teaspoon pepper
- ½ teaspoon salt
- 2 cups egg noodles
- 2 tablespoons parsley, freshly chopped
- 2 tablespoons lime juice (optional)

Directions

1. First, you need to prepare vegetables: dice up all of them into various sizes you prefer.
2. Heat 1 tablespoon of olive oil on medium heat and cook the chicken until browned on all sides, about 5 minutes. Remove the chicken and set it aside on a plate.
3. Sprinkle the pressure cooker pot with the other tablespoon of oil and add all the vegetables (onions, carrots, celery). Cook them for about 2 minutes stirring occasionally.
4. Meanwhile, the vegetables are cooking, cut the chicken into small pieces. Then add the broth, bay leaf, parsley, peas, corn, salt, and pepper. Add the noodles.
5. Return diced chicken to the pressure cooker, lock the lid, and bring the pot to pressure on high heat. Once the pressure cooker gets at pressure, reduce heat to the lowest level to maintain this pressure and cook for 8 minutes.
6. When cooked, carefully open the lid, season additionally with salt and pepper to taste, serve.

Dessert Recipes

Delicious Egg Custard

Preparation time: 4 minutes, cooking time: 7-8 minutes, servings: 4-6

Ingredients

- 4 cups skimmed milk
- 6 large eggs
- ¾ cup of sugar
- 1 teaspoon vanilla extract
- 1/8 teaspoon salt
- ¼ teaspoon cinnamon
- Fresh fruit, berries or nuts for garnish

Directions

1. In a large mixing bowl beat eggs. Pour milk, add sugar and season with salt and vanilla. Stir to combine evenly.

2. Pour the mixture into the Pressure Cooker safe bowl and cover a lid.
3. Add 1.5 cups of water to Pressure Cooker cooking pot and place trivet in bottom.
4. Place bowl on top of trivet.
5. Lock lid and close Pressure Valve and cook at High Pressure for 7 minutes.
6. When cooked, let the pressure release naturally for 10 minute.
7. Garnish with nuts, berries or other fruit, if desired.

Mouth-Watering Cinnamon Apple Pull Apart Bread

Preparation time: 5-7 minutes, cooking time: 22 minutes, servings: 3-5

Ingredients

- 3 middle-sized green apple, peeled and chopped
- 2 cans Pillsbury Cinnabon Cinnamon Rolls
- ¾ cup sugar
- 1½ teaspoons ground cinnamon
- ½ cup butter, melted
- A pinch of salt

Directions

1. In the mixing bowl combine cinnamon and sugar together and set aside.
2. Peel and chop apples and also set aside.
3. Open a separate your cinnamon rolls, put icing to the side. Cut into pie shapes. Each piece should have 4 pieces.

4. Toss apples and cinnamon rolls together with the cinnamon sugar and butter.
5. Put the mixture to the heat-proof pan.
6. Add 1 cup of water to the bottom of your pressure cooker. Place the pan into the pressure cooker, close and lock the lid and cook on high pressure for 20 minutes.
7. When cooked, use a quick release method for the pressure. Allow to chill.
8. Take a large plate and put it over your pot and flip to remove.
9. Pour the icing that came with the cinnamon rolls over the top of your bread.

5-Minute Delicious Applesauce

Preparation time: 5 minutes, cooking time: 5 minutes, servings: 4-6

Ingredients

- 10-12 large organic apples, peeled and quartered
- 2 tablespoon pasture butter
- 1 tablespoon ground cinnamon
- 1 tablespoon light colored honey
- Fresh juice of 1/2 lemon
- ¼ teaspoon salt
- 1 cup water

Directions

1. First, you need to prepare the apples. Wash and peel them. Cut into quarters and place into the pressure cooker bowl. Add butter, cinnamon, honey, salt and water into the cooker bowl with the apples.
2. Put the lid on and secure it in the locked position.
3. Take the pressure cooker to a high pressure and cook for 4-5 minutes.

4. When timer beeps, reduce the pressure using a natural pressure release.
5. Carefully remove the lid and check out the beauty inside of the pot.
6. Ladle apples into a high powered blender or food processor. If there is a lot of excess liquid leftover in the pressure cooker bowl, only use about half of the liquid. Pulse just until fully combined and smooth.
7. Enjoy warm or cold.

Simple Caramel Flan

Preparation time: 7 minutes, cooking time: 10 minutes, servings: 4-6

Ingredients

- 4 large eggs
- 1 can sweetened condensed milk
- 1 cup skimmed milk
- ¾ cup water
- 1 teaspoon vanilla extract
- A pinch of salt
- ½ cup maple syrup

Directions

1. Take the large mixing bowl and beat eggs. Pour in condensed and skimmed milk, water, add vanilla extract; season with salt.
2. Pour thin layer of maple syrup across several pressure cooker safe ramekins or baking dish.

3. Pour egg mixture over maple syrup layer until ramekins are slightly more than 3/4 full. Cover tops with aluminum foil.
4. Put one cup water in your pressure cooker and set a trivet. Stack two layers of ramekins, making sure to stay below the fill line.
5. Set Manual High Pressure and cook for 9 minutes.
6. Once the timer beeps, allow resting for 10 minutes before releasing any remaining pressure and then removing ramekins.
7. Cool slightly and enjoy, or it will be better to refrigerate for several hours if you can restrain yourself.

Cooking Measurement Conversions

Liquid Measures

1 gal = 4 qt = 8 pt = 16 cups = 128 fl oz
½ gal = 2 qt = 4 pt = 8 cups = 64 fl oz
¼ gal = 1 qt = 2 pt = 4 cups = 32 fl oz
½ qt = 1 pt = 2 cups = 16 fl oz
¼ qt = ½ pt = 1 cup = 8 fl oz

Dry Measures

1 cup = 16 Tbsp = 48 tsp = 250ml
¾ cup = 12 Tbsp = 36 tsp = 175ml
⅔ cup = 10 ⅔ Tbsp = 32 tsp = 150ml
½ cup = 8 Tbsp = 24 tsp = 125ml
⅓ cup = 5 ⅓ Tbsp = 16 tsp = 75ml
¼ cup = 4 Tbsp = 12 tsp = 50ml
⅛ cup = 2 Tbsp = 6 tsp = 30ml
1 Tbsp = 3 tsp = 15ml

Dash or Pinch or Speck = less than ⅛ tsp

Quickies

1 fl oz = 30 ml
1 oz = 28.35 g
1 lb = 16 oz (454 g)
1 kg = 2.2 lb
1 quart = 2 pints

U.S.	Canadian
¼ tsp	1.25 mL
½ tsp	2.5 mL
1 tsp	5 mL
1 Tbl	15 mL
¼ cup	50 mL
⅓ cup	75 mL
½ cup	125 mL
⅔ cup	150 mL
¾ cup	175 mL
1 cup	250 mL
1 quart	1 liter

Recipe Abbreviations

Cup = c or C
Fluid = fl
Gallon = gal
Ounce = oz
Package = pkg
Pint = pt
Pound = lb or #
Quart = qt
Square = sq
Tablespoon = T or Tbl or TBSP or TBS
Teaspoon = t or tsp

*Some measurements were rounded

Fahrenheit (°F) to Celcius (°C)

°C = (°F - 32) x 5/9

°F	°C
32°F	0°C
40°F	4°C
140°F	60°C
150°F	65°C
160°F	70°C
225°F	107°C
250°F	121°C
275°F	135°C
300°F	150°C
325°F	165°C
350°F	177°C
375°F	190°C
400°F	205°C
425°F	220°C
450°F	230°C
475°F	245°C
500°F	260°C

OVEN TEMPERATURES

WARMING: 200°F
VERY SLOW: 250°F - 275°F
SLOW: 300°F - 325°F
MODERATE: 350°F - 375°F
HOT: 400°F - 425°F
VERY HOT: 450°F - 475°F

Copyright 2016 by Katy Adams - All rights reserved.

No part of this publication may be reproduced or transmitted in any form or by any means, mechanical or electronic, including photocopying and recording, or by any information storage and retrieval system, without permission, in written, from the author.

All attempts have been made to verify information provided in this publication. Neither the author nor the publisher assumes any responsibility for errors or omissions of the subject matter herein. This publication is not intended for use as a source of legal or accounting advice. The Publisher wants to stress that the information contained herein may be subject to varying state and/or local laws or regulations. All users are advised to retain competent counsel to determine what state and/or local laws or regulations may apply to the user's particular business.

The purchaser or reader of this publication assumes responsibility for the use of these materials and information. Adherence to all applicable laws and regulations, federal, state, and local, governing professional licensing, business practices, advertising, and all other aspects of doing business in the United States or any other jurisdiction is the sole responsibility of the purchaser or reader.

The author and Publisher assume no responsibility or liability whatsoever on the behalf of any purchaser or reader of these materials for injury due to use of any of the methods contained herein. Any perceived slights of specific people or organizations are unintentional.

Conclusion

Thank you again for downloading my cookbook! I Hope this book helps you to know more interesting and tasty recipes or inspire you to create your own unique dishes.

Made in the USA
Lexington, KY
04 January 2017